BREATHS
OF
AYR

*An entertaining selection
of the pithiest and most memorable lines
from the works of Robert Burns*

compiled by
David Vallance

Printed by
Walker & Connell Ltd., Hastings Square, Darvel, Ayrshire, Scotland
1993

INTRODUCTION

A number of sayings of Robert Burns, because of their aptness and pungency, have now found worldwide usage. However, the student of Robert Burns knows that these still represent only a very small fraction of the gems for which he was responsible. The more I read Burns' works, the more impressed I have become by the wealth of pithy, quotable lines in them; he is indeed the master of the encapsulated truth. Again and again he hits the nail on the head regarding our human experience.

We marvel how, in such a short life, it was possible to acquire an understanding of human nature so wide and so profound. His attitude to people and events was direct, passionate and uncompromising. This is why he hates and loves, laughs and mourns, condemns and praises, with a vigour peculiarly his own. His interests and sympathies encompass almost every aspect of humanity. He writes of individual feelings and people but also of public events; he castigates hypocrisy but still retains faith in ideals; he denounces injustice and other social evils but does not lose trust in Providence and the goodness of the human heart. All his comments on society and individuals are based on an all-embracing version of 'Nature's social union', and on his own sheer love of life and people. This is why his thoughts still have relevance when quoted today.

Amongst the categories in this collection the reader will look in vain for one entitled 'humour'. This is because the humour in the works of Burns is so widespread that it is difficult to separate. What can one do about a writer who paradoxically infuses hilarity into the dying words of a pet sheep; and who, tongue in cheek, extols the miraculous powers of what others would call a mealy pudding? Then there is the incomparable satire and withering scorn of 'Holy Willie', before the Bard transforms himself into an arch maiden for 'The Braw Wooer'. These are but examples.

In this selection, however, the reader will find expressed love, loyalty, hate, tenderness, grief, remorse, scorn and, in fact, most of the emotions to which human beings are subject.

Many of Burn's earlier poems, particularly those addressed to friends, were evidently not written for publication. Writing in rhyme came naturally to him, as well as providing practice in his craft of poetry. What ultimately makes Burns' thoughts so memorable, and so quotable, is the easy grace of expression and striking turn of phrase. In this selection, a few little-used words in the Scottish dialect have been given an explanatory note, and slight cuts and alterations have been made in some quotations in the interests of brevity and point. For such reasons, I trust these will be acceptable to the reader.

Anyone who has the temerity to bring out a selection of quotations, or anything else, cannot expect to please everyone. But if the reader finds in these pages something to amuse, something to provoke thought, something liked already, and something fresh and memorable, that is the intention. If it excites new interest and pleasure in the works of Robert Burns, so much the better.

INDEX

E'en then, a wish (I mind its pow'r),
A wish that to my latest hour
Shall strongly heave my breast,
That I for poor auld Scotland's sake
Some usefu' plan or book could make,
Or sing a sang at least.

CONVIVIALITY

*They had been fou'
for weeks thegither.*

*If we lead a life of pleasure,
'Tis no matter how or where!*

•

*Let them prate about decorum,
Who have character to lose.*

The Jolly Beggars CW 191

♦ ♦ ♦

*Love blinks, Wit slaps, an social Mirth
Forgets there's Care upo the earth.*

The Twa Dogs CW 143

♦ ♦ ♦

Freedom and whisky gang thegither

The Author's Earnest Cry and Lament CW 179

♦ ♦ ♦

It never fails, on drinkin deep,
to ¹kittle up our notion.   tickle

♦

There's some are fou o love divine;
There's some are fou o brandy.

♦

And monie jobs that day begin,
May end in ¹houghmagandie.   fornication

The Holy Fair CW 137/9

♦ ♦ ♦

Cold-pausing Caution's lesson scorning,
We frisk away.

Epistle to James Smith CW 171

♦ ♦ ♦

¹Syne we'll sit down an take our ²whitter   Then, liquor
To cheer our heart;
An faith, we'se be acquainted better
Before we part.

♦

But ye whom social pleasure charms . . . . .
Come to my bowl, come to my arms,
My friends, my brothers!

Epistle to J Lapraik CW 103/4

♦ ♦ ♦

7

I was na fou, but just had plenty.

Death and Doctor Hornbook CW 96

◆ ◆ ◆

We think na on the lang Scots miles . . . . .
That lie between us and our hame.

◆

Tam ¹lo'ed him like a very brither;   loved
They had been fou for weeks thegither.

◆

Care, mad to see a man sae happy,
E'en drown'd himsel amang the ¹nappy.   ale

◆

As bees flee hame wi lades o treasure,
The minutes wing'd their way wi pleasure.

◆

Kings may be blest but Tam was glorious,
O'er a' the ills o life victorious.

◆

But pleasures are like poppies spread;
You seize the flow'r, its bloom is shed.

◆

Inspiring bold John Barleycorn
What dangers thou canst make us scorn!

Tam o' Shanter CW 410/12

◆ ◆ ◆

To sum up all: be merry, I advise;
And as we're merry, may we still be wise.

Address Spoken by Miss Fontenelle CW 509

◆ ◆ ◆

Thou shalt find . . . .
Friendship, virtue, every grace,
Dwelling in this happy place.

At Whigham's Inn, Sanquhar CW 350

◆ ◆ ◆

The greybeard, old Wisdom,
may boast of his treasures . . . .
But Folly has raptures to give.

Lines written on window of the Globe Tavern CW 568

◆ ◆ ◆

Let Meg now take away the flesh,
And Jock bring in the spirit.

Grace Before and After Meat CW 409

◆ ◆ ◆

And still the more and more they drank,
Their joy did more abound.

John Barleycorn CW 61

◆ ◆ ◆

For ale and brandy's stars and moon,
And blude-red wine's the risin sun.

◆

9

But here we're a' in ae accord, one
For ¹ilka man that's drunk's a lord. every

Guidwife, Count the Lawin CW 441

•••

O, guid ale comes, and guid ale goes . . . .
Guid ale keeps my heart ¹aboon. on high

O Guid Ale Comes CW 598

•••

We'll tak a cup o kindness yet,
For auld lang syne.

Auld Lang Syne CW 341

PHILOSOPHY

Rejoiced they were not men but dogs.

Life is all a variorum,
We regard not how it goes.

The Jolly Beggars CW 191

◆ ◆ ◆

When up they gat, an shook their lugs,
Rejoic'd they were na men, but dogs.

The Twa Dogs CW 146

◆ ◆ ◆

This life, sae far's I understand,
Is a' enchanted fairy-land.

Epistle to James Smith CW 171

◆ ◆ ◆

But facts are ¹chiels that winna ²ding,   fellows, yield,
An ¹downa be disputed.   cannot

A Dream CW 234

11

The best-laid schemes o mice an men
Gang aft agley.

To a Mouse CW 132

♦ ♦ ♦

However Fortune kick the ba',
Has ay some cause to smile.

♦

Then let us cheerfu' acquiesce,
Nor make our scanty pleasures less
By pining at our state.

♦

And even should misfortunes come . . . .
They ¹gie the wit of age to youth; give
They let us ¹ken oursel. know

Epistle to Davie, a Brother Poet CW 87/88

♦ ♦ ♦

O Life! thou art a galling load,
Along a rough, a weary road.

Despondency CW 207

♦ ♦ ♦

`O Man! while in thy early years,
How prodigal of time!

♦

The poor, oppressed, honest man
Had never, sure, been born,
Had there not been some recompense
To comfort those that mourn!

Man was Made to Mourn CW 123/5

◆ ◆ ◆

Ne'er mind how Fortune waft an warp;
She's but a bitch.

◆

The social, friendly, honest man,
Whate'er he be,
Tis he fulfils great Nature's plan,
And none but he.

Second Epistle to J Lapraik CW 105/6

◆ ◆ ◆

Folk maun do something for their bread,
An sae ¹maun Death.   must

Death and Doctor Hornbook CW 97

◆ ◆ ◆

Affliction's sons are brothers in distress.

A Winter Night CW 260

◆ ◆ ◆

There ruminate with sober thought,
On all thou'st seen, and heard, and wrought.

◆

13

Did thy fortune ebb or flow?
Did many talents gild thy span?
Or frugal Nature grudge thee one?

◆

Thus resign'd and quiet, creep
To the bed of lasting sleep.

Written in Friars Carse Hermitage CW 325/6

◆ ◆ ◆

Nae man can tether time or tide.

Tam o'Shanter CW 411

◆ ◆ ◆

Life is but a day at most,
Sprung from night in darkness lost.

Verses in Friars Carse Hermitage CW 324

◆ ◆ ◆

Tho Fortune's road be rough an hilly . . . .
We never heed,
But take it like the uncrack'd filly,
Proud o her speed.

Epistle to Major Logan CW 256

◆ ◆ ◆

Instinct's a brute, and Sentiment a fool!

Epistle to Robert Graham, Esq of Fintry CW 332

◆ ◆ ◆

Though humble he who gives,
Rich is the tribute of the grateful mind.

To Miss Graham of Fintry CW 511

◆ ◆ ◆

Since life's gay scenes must charm no more
Still much is left behind . . . . .
The comforts of the mind.

Inscription . . . . to Chloris CW 557

◆ ◆ ◆

That, whether doing, suffering, or forbearing,
You may do miracles by persevering.

Prologue Spoken at the Theatre of Dumfries CW 377

◆ ◆ ◆

A knave and fool are plants of every soil.

Scots Prologue for Mrs Sutherland CW 399

◆ ◆ ◆

Laugh in Misfortune's face - the beldam witch-
Say, you'll be merry tho you can't be rich!

Address Spoken by Miss Fontenelle CW 509

◆ ◆ ◆

Then know this truth, ye Sons of Men . . . .
Your darkest terrors may be vain,
Your brightest hopes may fail!

Ode on the Departed Regency Bill CW 354

◆ ◆ ◆

Good Lord, what is Man . . . .
All in all he's a problem must puzzle the Devil.

Inscribed to the Rt Hon C J Fox CW 357

◆ ◆ ◆

Ask why God made the gem so small,
And why so huge the granite?
Because God meant mankind should set
That higher value on it.

Epigram on Miss Davies CW 491

◆ ◆ ◆

Thus ev'ry kind their pleasure find,
The savage and the tender.

Now Westlin Winds CW 44

◆ ◆ ◆

Come weel, come woe, I ¹care na by;   do not care
I'll tak what Heav'n will send me.

My Nanie, O CW 46

◆ ◆ ◆

O what is death but parting breath?

Macpherson's Farewell CW 308

◆ ◆ ◆

As ye ¹maut, so ²maun ye brew.   malt, must

As I Went Out ae May Morning CW 466

◆ ◆ ◆

16

Time but th'impression stronger makes,
As streams their channels deeper wear.

Thou Lingering Star CW 373

• • •

Chords that vibrate sweetest pleasure
Thrill the deepest notes of woe.

On Sensibility CW 402

• • •

Thou golden time o youthfu prime,
Why comes thou not again?

The Winter of Life CW 525

• • •

Contented wi little, and ¹cantie wi ²mair. happy more

Contented wi Little CW 531

• • •

Ye are sae grave, nae doubt ye're wise.

Epistle to James Smith CW 173

• • •

Let Fortune's wheel at random rin,
And fools may ¹tyne, and knaves may win! lose

Philly and Willy CW 530

LOVE

His cheek to her's he aft did lay.

Ye wingèd Hours that o'er us pass'd,
Enraptur'd more the more enjoy'd.

The Lament CW 205

◆ ◆ ◆

Lang syne in Eden's ¹bonie yard,   garden
When youthfu lovers first were pair'd ....
The raptur'd hour.

Address to the Deil CW 163

◆ ◆ ◆

Wi kindly bleat, when she did spy him,
She ran wi speed.   Pet Ewe
Poor Maillie's Elegy CW 64

◆ ◆ ◆

I see the Sire of Love on high,
And own His work indeed divine!

Address to Edinburgh CW 263

◆ ◆ ◆

The liquid fire of strong desire,
I've poured it in each bosom.

Nature's Law CW 253

◆ ◆ ◆

I ¹ken't her heart was a' my ain;   knew
I lov'd her most sincerely.

The Rigs O Barley CW 49

◆ ◆ ◆

Let Fortune's gifts at random flee . . . .
Supremely blest wi love and thee.

The Birks of Aberfeldie CW 289

◆ ◆ ◆

A man may kiss a bonie lass,
And ay be welcome back again!

Duncan Davison CW 311

◆ ◆ ◆

I care na thy daddie, his lands and his money . . . .
But sae that thou'lt hae me for better or waur.

Sweet Tibbie Dunbar CW 381

◆ ◆ ◆

A ringlet of thy flowing hair,
I'll wear it still for ever mair.

Where Helen Lies CW 311

♦ ♦ ♦

Sleep I can get nane
For thinkin on my dearie.

Ay Waukin, O CW 382

♦ ♦ ♦

He gaz'd, he wish'd,
He fear'd, he blush'd,
And trembled where he stood.

♦

A faltering, ardent kiss he stole . . . .
And sigh'd his very soul.

On a Bank of Flowers CW 385

♦ ♦ ♦

But blessings on your frosty ¹pow, head
John Anderson my ¹jo! dear

John Anderson my Jo CW 391

♦ ♦ ♦

Till clay-cauld death sall blin' my e'e,
Ye sall be my dearie.

Ca' the Yowes to the Knowes CW 300

♦ ♦ ♦

Deep in heart-wrung tears I'll pledge thee.

Ae Fond Kiss CW 434

Tak this frae me, my bonie ¹hen;   dear
It's plenty ¹beets the luver's fire!   fans

◆

Content and love brings peace and joy;
What ¹mair ²hae Queens upon a throne? more, have
The Country Lass CW 455/6

◆ ◆ ◆

And ¹ilka bird sang o its luve,   every
And fondly sae did I o mine.

The Banks o' Doon C. W. 420

◆ ◆ ◆

My luve is like the melodie,
That's sweetly play'd in tune.

◆

And I will luve thee still, my dear,
Till a' the seas gang dry.

◆

And I will come again, my luve,
Tho it were ten thousand mile!

A Red, Red Rose CW 517

◆ ◆ ◆

Gif ye hae onie luve for me,
O wrang na my virginitie!
The Lass that made the Bed to Me CW 584

◆ ◆ ◆

The golden hours on angel wings
Flew o'er me and my dearie.

Highland Mary CW 470

◆ ◆ ◆

But when she charms my sight . . . .
'Tis then I wake to life and joy!

Sleep'st Thou CW 526

◆ ◆ ◆

Those smiles and glances let me see,
That makes the miser's treasure poor.

Mary Morison CW 69

◆ ◆ ◆

The sweets of love are wash'd with tears.

The Primrose CW 502

◆ ◆ ◆

The desert were a Paradise
If thou wert there.

O, Wert Thou in the Cauld Blast CW 567

◆ ◆ ◆

His cheek to hers he aft did lay,
And love was ay the tale.

As Down the Burn CW 501

WOMEN

Our sulky sullen dame.

The soul o' life, the heaven below

The saul o life, the heav'n below,   soul
Is rapture-giving Woman.

To the Guidwife of Wauchope House CW 272

◆ ◆ ◆

O, how that Name inspires my style!   My Jean
The words come ¹skelpin rank an file,   racing
¹Amaist before I ken!   almost

Epistle to Davie, a Brother Poet CW 89

◆ ◆ ◆

Sweet female Beauty hand in hand with Spring.

The Brigs of Ayr CW 249

◆ ◆ ◆

Whare sits our sulky, sullen dame . . . .
Nursing her wrath to keep it warm.

Tam o' Shanter CW 410

O Tam, had'st thou but been sae wise,
As ¹taen thy ²ain wife Kate's advice!   taken, own

♦

Ah! gentle dames, it ¹gars me ²greet,   makes, cry
To think how monie counsels sweet . . . .
The husband frae the wife despises!

Tam o' Shanter CW 410/11

♦ ♦ ♦

Does the sober bed of marriage
Witness brighter scenes of love?

The Jolly Beggars CW 191

♦ ♦ ♦

Curs'd be the man, the poorest wretch in life,
The crouching vassal to the tyrant wife!

♦

I'd charm her with the magic of a switch,
I'd kiss her maids, and kick the perverse bitch.

The Henpecked Husband CW 610

♦ ♦ ♦

We married men, how oft we find
The best of things will tire us!

On Marriage CW 608

♦ ♦ ♦

Here lies a man a woman ruled-
The Devil ruled the woman.

Epitaph on a Henpecked Squire CW 209

♦ ♦ ♦

Her prentice han' she try'd on man,   Nature
And then she made the lasses.

Green Grow the Rashes, O   CW 81

♦ ♦ ♦

But warily ¹tent when ye come to court me . . . heed
Come up the back-style, and let naebody see.

♦

Gang by me as tho' that ye car'd na a flie,
But steal me a blink o' your bonie black e'e.

♦

Ay vow and protest that ye care na for me . . . .
But court na anither tho jokin ye be.

Whistle An I'll Come To You, My Lad   CW 496

♦ ♦ ♦

I'm o'er young, 'twad be a sin
To tak me frae my mammie yet.

I'm o'er Young to Marry Yet   CW 307

♦ ♦ ♦

His ¹gear may buy him glens and ²knowes;   money
                                             hillocks
But me he shall not buy nor ¹fee.   hire

♦

Wi' his teethless ¹gab and his auld ²beld pow .   mouth
                                                .bald
That auld man shall never ¹daunton me!   master

To Daunton Me   CW 316

If that she be bony, I shall think her right;
If that she be ugly, where's the odds at night?

Broom Besoms CW 610

◆ ◆ ◆

Her lips, still as she fragrant breath'd,
It richer dyed the rose.

On a Bank of Flowers CW 385

◆ ◆ ◆

Meg was meek, and Meg was mild,
Sweet and harmless as a child;
Wiser men than me's beguil'd-

Whistle o'er the Lave o't CW 335

◆ ◆ ◆

His blude it is frozen
O, dreary's the night wi a crazy auld man!

What Can a Young Lassie CW 441

◆ ◆ ◆

Wit and Grace and Love and Beauty
In ae constellation shine!

Bonnie Wee Thing CW 447

◆ ◆ ◆

And lassie, ye're but young, ye ken!
Then wait a wee, and ¹cannie ²wale.   carefully choose

◆

Syne as ye brew, my maiden fair,{sup}1{/sup}   then
*Keep mind that ye *{sup}1{/sup}*maun drink the *{sup}2{/sup}*yill!*   must, ale
The Country Lass CW 455/6

♦ ♦ ♦

{sup}1{/sup}Sic a wife as Willie had,   such
*I *{sup}1{/sup}*wad na gie a button for her.*   wouldn't give
Willie Wastle CW 459

♦ ♦ ♦

*I hae been a Devil the *{sup}1{/sup}*feck o my life . . . .*   most
But ne'er was in Hell till I met wi a wife.
Kellyburn Braes CW 462

♦ ♦ ♦

On peace an rest my mind was bent,
And, fool I was! I married!
O, Ay My Wife, she Dang me CW 597

♦ ♦ ♦

Why then ask of silly man
To oppose great Nature's plan?
We'll be constant, while we can . . . .
Let not Women e'er Complain CW 525

♦ ♦ ♦

And still to her charms she alone is a stranger:
Her modest demeanour's the jewel of a'.
Young Jessie CW 486

♦ ♦ ♦

27

The brightest o Beauty may cloy when possess'd.

A Lass Wi a Tocher CW 563

◆ ◆ ◆

I said there was naething I hated like men . . . .
The Lord forgie me for ¹liein.

lying

◆

So e'en to preserve the poor body in life,
I think I ¹maun wed him tomorrow!

must

The Braw Wooer CW 555/6

◆ ◆ ◆

The sweetest flower that deck'd the mead,
Now trodden like the vilest weed -
Let simple maid the lesson read.

O, let me in this ae Night CW 539

BENEDICTION

Thine be ilka joy and treasure.

Long may thy hardy sons of rustic toil
Be blest with health, and peace, and sweet content!

The Cotter's Saturday Night CW 151

❖ ❖ ❖

So may his flock increase, an grow   a Pet Ewe speaks
To scores o lambs, an packs o woo'!

The Death and Dying Words of Poor Maillie CW 63

❖ ❖ ❖

Heav'n mak you guid as weel as ¹*braw,*   fair
An' gie you lads a-plenty.

A Dream CW 236

❖ ❖ ❖

This life has joys for you and I;
And joys that riches ne'er could buy.

Epistle to Davie, a Brother Poet CW 88

◆ ◆ ◆

Accept this tribute from the Bard
Thou brought from Fortune's mirkest gloom.

•

But I'll remember thee, Glencairn,
And a' that thou hast done for me!

Lament for James, Earl of Glencairn CW 425

◆ ◆ ◆

Ye Powers of peace and peaceful song,
Look down with gracious eyes.

Nature's Law CW 254

◆ ◆ ◆

Our guidwife's wee birdie cock . . . .
has nae sic breedin,
But better stuff ne'er claw'd a [1]midden.   dung heap

Elegy on the Year 1788 CW 347

◆ ◆ ◆

Heaven spare you lang to kiss the breath
o' mony flow'ry simmers.

•

An may he wear an auld man's beard,
A credit to his country!

To Mr McAdam of Craigen-Gillan CW 274

Farewell, then! lang ¹hale then,   health
An plenty be your ¹fa'!   lot

◆

May losses and crosses
Ne'er at your ¹hallan ²ca'!   portal call

To the Guidwife of Wauchope House CW 272

◆ ◆ ◆

I lay my hand upon my swelling breast,
And grateful would, but cannot, speak the rest.

Sonnet to Robert Graham, Esq., of Fintry C. W. 362

◆ ◆ ◆

So may no ruffian feeling in thy breast . . . .
But Peace attune thy gentle soul to rest.

To Miss Graham of Fintry CW 511

◆ ◆ ◆

No wrinkle furrow'd by the hand of care,
Nor ever sorrow, add one silver hair!

On John McMurdo CW 356

◆ ◆ ◆

Yet, tho his caustic wit was biting rude,
His heart was warm, benevolent, and good.

William Smellie - a Sketch CW 433

◆ ◆ ◆

Who is proof to thy personal converse and wit,
Is proof to all other temptation.

Apology For Declining An Invitation To Dine CW 560

A warmer heart Death ne'er made cold.
Epitaph for Robert Aiken, Esq CW 71

◆ ◆ ◆

If there's another world, he lives in bliss;
If there is none, he made the best of this.
Epitaph on William Muir in Tarbolton Mill CW 70

◆ ◆ ◆

Bairns . . . . O, tread ye lightly on his grass -
Perhaps he was your father!
Epitaph for a Wag in Mauchline CW 231

◆ ◆ ◆

If such Thou refusest admission above,
Then whom wilt Thou favour, Good God?
Epitaph on Robert Muir CW 322

◆ ◆ ◆

And may those pleasures gild thy reign
That ne'er wad blink on mine!
Lament of Mary Queen of Scots CW 401

◆ ◆ ◆

The friend of man - to vice alone a foe;
For ev'n his failings lean'd to virtue's side.
Epitaph On My Honoured Father CW 71

◆ ◆ ◆

Thine be ilka joy and treasure,
Peace, Enjoyment, Love and Pleasure!
Ae Fond Kiss CW 434

ADVICE

*Mind to be kind
to ane anither.*

*An when you think upo your mither,
Mind to be kind to ane anither.*
The Death and Dying Words of Poor Maillie CW 64

◆ ◆ ◆

*Aye free, aff han', your story tell,
When wi a bosom cronie;
But still keep something to yoursel
Ye scarcely tell to onie.*

◆

*But [1]keek thro ev'ry other man,
Wi' sharpen'd, sly inspection.*

peep

◆

To catch Dame Fortune's golden smile,
Assiduous wait upon her.

•

And gather gear by ev'ry wile
That's justify'd by honor.

•

And may ye better ¹reck the ²rede,   heed, advice
Than ever did th' adviser!

Epistle to a Young Friend CW 221/3

• • •

Hope not sunshine ev'ry hour,
Fear not clouds will always lour.

Written in Friars Carse Hermitage CW 325

• • •

Whene'er to drink you are inclin'd,
Or ¹cutty ²sarks rin in your mind,   short vests
Think! ye may buy the joys o'er dear.

Tam o' Shanter CW 415

• • •

Thou whom chance may hither lead . . . .
Grave these maxims on thy soul.

•

Happiness is but a name,
Make content and ease thy aim.

•

But, thy utmost duly done,
Welcome what thou can'st not shun.

34

◆

Keep the name of Man in mind,
And dishonour not thy kind.

Verses in Friars Carse Hermitage CW 324

◆ ◆ ◆

A great man's smile, ye ken fu well,
Is ay a blest infection.

To Mr McAdam of Craigen-Gillan CW 274

◆ ◆ ◆

Tell the sore prest sons of Care,
Never, never to despair.

Ode on the Departed Regency Bill CW 353

◆ ◆ ◆

Would thou hae Nobles' patronage?
First learn to live without it.

On some Commemorations of Thomson CW 422

◆ ◆ ◆

A man may drink, and no be drunk;
A man may fight, and no be slain.

Duncan Davison CW 311

◆ ◆ ◆

Tak this advice o me, bony lass,
Humility wad set thee best.

As I cam down by yon Castle Wa' CW 443

◆ ◆ ◆

O guid advisement comes nae ill.

The Country Lass CW 455

Then catch the moments as they fly . . . .
Believe me, Happiness is shy!

Here's a Bottle CW 608

◆ ◆ ◆

Know, prudent, cautious, self-control
Is wisdom's root.

A Bard's Epitaph CW 220

DISFAVOUR

*Curse thou his basket
and his store.*

May gravels round his ¹blather wrench,   bladder
An gouts torment him, inch by inch.

Scotch Drink CW 167

◆◆◆

'Gie dreeping roasts to countra lairds,
Till icicles hing frae their beards.

Epistle to James Smith CW 172

◆◆◆

A set o dull, conceited ¹hashes   wasters
Confuse their brains in college-classes;
They gang in ¹stirks, and come out asses.   bullocks

Epistle to J Lapraik CW 102

◆◆◆

37

But this that I am gaun to tell,
Is just as true's the Deil's in Hell.

Death and Doctor Hornbook CW 96

◆ ◆ ◆

With order, symmetry, or taste unblest . . . .
The craz'd creations of misguided whim.

The Brigs of Ayr CW 247

◆ ◆ ◆

The Rigid Righteous is a fool,
The Rigid Wise anither.

Address to the Unco Guid CW 74

◆ ◆ ◆

See these hands, ne'er stretched to save,
Hands that took, but never gave.

Ode, Sacred to the Memory of Mrs Oswald CW 343

◆ ◆ ◆

Critics . . . . Those cut-throat bandits
in the paths of fame.

To Robert Graham, Esq., of Fintry CW 431

◆ ◆ ◆

Curse Thou his basket and his store,
Kail an potatoes!

Holy Willie's Prayer CW 94

◆ ◆ ◆

My curse upon your venom'd stang,
That shoots my tortur'd gums alang.

Address to the Toothache CW 553

◆ ◆ ◆

We seek but little, Lord, from Thee:
Thou kens we get as little!

A New Psalm for the Chapel of Kilmarnock CW 355

◆ ◆ ◆

From liberty how angels fell,
That now are galley-slaves in Hell

On Glenriddell's Fox Breaking his Chain CW 426

◆ ◆ ◆

Banknote - [1]*Wae* [2]*worth thy power,*   woe befall
thou cursed leaf!

Lines Written on a Banknote CW 223

◆ ◆ ◆

O burning Hell! in all thy store of torments
There's not a keener lash!   of Guilt

Remorse CW 66

◆ ◆ ◆

An idiot race, to honour lost -
Who know them best despise them most. The Hanoverians

Written by Somebody on the Window CW 286

◆ ◆ ◆

O Death, it's my opinion,
Thou ne'er took such a ¹bleth'rin bitch   babbling
Into thy dark dominion.

Epitaph on a Noisy Polemic CW 70

◆ ◆ ◆

(He) hopes to get salvation;
But if such as he in Heav'n may be,
Then welcome - hail! damnation.

Epitaph on James Grieve CW 67

◆ ◆ ◆

'In his skull there's a famine,'
a starved reptile cries;
'And his heart, it is poison!' another replies.

Epitaph on Mr. Walter Riddell CW 516

◆ ◆ ◆

Dame Nature call'd to Death . . . .
'How shall I make a fool again?,
My choicest model thou hast ¹taen.'   taken

On Wm. Graham, Esq., of Mossknowe CW 522

◆ ◆ ◆

This worthless body damned himsel
To save the Lord the trouble.

On a Suicide CW 521

◆ ◆ ◆

40

Tho ye do little ¹skaith ....   harm
And gif ye canna bite, ye may bark.

The Kirk's Alarm CW 360

◆ ◆ ◆

It's a' for the apple he'll nourish the tree,
It's a' for the hiney he'll cherish the bee!

My Tocher's the Jewel CW 440

◆ ◆ ◆

Her face ¹wad fyle the Logan Water.   would foul

Willie Wastle CW 459

INTROSPECTION

I sat me down to ponder.

But what could ye other expect,
Of ane that's avowedly daft?

The Jolly Beggars CW 185

◆◆◆

I'll wander on, wi tentless heed . . . .   careless
Till Fate shall snap the brittle thread.

For me, an aim I never ¹fash;   bother with
I rhyme for fun.

But give me real, sterling wit,
And I'm content.

I'll sit down o'er my scanty meal . . . .
Wi cheerfu face,
As lang's the Muses dinna fail
To say the grace.

◆

I ¹jouk beneath Misfortune's blows   dodge
As weel's I may.

Epistle to James Smith CW 170/3

◆ ◆ ◆

How I had spent my youthfu prime . . . .
But stringing ¹blethers up in rhyme,   nonsense
For fools to sing.

◆

To swear . . . .
That I henceforth would be rhyme-proof
Till my last breath.

The Vision CW 115

◆ ◆ ◆

With Woe I nightly vigils keep . . . .
And mourn, in lamentation deep,
How life and love are all a dream!

The Lament CW 204

◆ ◆ ◆

I, listless yet restless,
Find ev'ry prospect vain.

◆

43

But ah! those pleasures, loves, and joys,
Which I too keenly taste.

•

O enviable early days . . . .
To care, to guilt unknown!

Despondency CW 207/8

♦ ♦ ♦

If I'm design'd yon lordling's slave . . . .
Why was an independent wish
E'er planted in my mind?

Man was made to Mourn CW 124

♦ ♦ ♦

The leafless trees my fancy please,
Their fate resembles mine!

Winter: a Dirge CW 51

♦ ♦ ♦

Thou know'st that Thou hast formed me
With passions wild and strong.

A Prayer in the Prospect of Death CW 54

♦ ♦ ♦

Perhaps it may turn out a sang;
Perhaps, turn out a sermon.

Epistle to a Young Friend CW 221

♦ ♦ ♦

44

[1]Amaist as soon as I could spell,
I to the [1]crambo-jingle fell;
Tho rude an rough.

Almost

rhyming verse

♦

Gie me ae spark o Nature's fire,
That's a' the learning I desire.

♦

My Muse, tho' hamely in attire,
May touch the heart.

♦

There's ae wee faut they whyles lay to me,
I like the lasses - Gude forgie me!

Epistle to J Lapraik CW 102/3

♦ ♦ ♦

With that controlling pow'r assist ev'n me,
Those headlong furious passions to confine.

Stanzas on the same Occasion CW 55

♦ ♦ ♦

Poetic ardors in my bosom swell.

Verses Written with a Pencil CW 288

♦ ♦ ♦

God knows, I'm no the thing I should be,
Nor am I even the thing I could be.

Epistle to the Rev. John McMath CW 130

♦ ♦ ♦

45

I fear unless ye geld me,
I'll ne'er be better!

Reply to a Trimming Epistle received from a Tailor CW 243

◆ ◆ ◆

I mind it weel, in early date,
When I was beardless, young and ¹blate . .   shy
Yet ¹unco proud to learn.   very

◆

I mind . . . When first amang the yellow corn
A man I reckon'd was.

◆

But still the elements o sang
In formless jumble, right an' wrang,
Wild floated in my brain.

To the Guidwife of Wauchope House CW 271

◆ ◆ ◆

Ere my poor soul such deep damnation stain,
My horny fist assume the plough again!

Epistle to Robert Graham, Esq., of Fintry CW 332

◆ ◆ ◆

Then farewell folly, hide and hair o't,
For ance and ay!

To Collector Mitchell CW 562

◆ ◆ ◆

Ah, woe is me, my Mother dear!
A man of strife ye've born me.

Ah, Woe is Me, my Mother Dear CW 209

◆ ◆ ◆

All villain as I am - a damned wretch . . . .
Still my heart melts at human wretchedness.

Tragic Fragment CW 46

◆ ◆ ◆

I've little to spend and naething to lend,
But devil a shilling I awe.

The Ronalds of the Bennals CW 78

◆ ◆ ◆

Up in the morning's no for me,
Up in the morning early!

Up in the Morning Early CW 310

◆ ◆ ◆

I gaed a ¹waefu gate yestreen,   went a woeful way
A gate I fear I'll dearly rue.

The Blue-Eyed Lassie CW 333

◆ ◆ ◆

I'll count my health my greatest wealth
Sae lang as I'll enjoy it.

Here's to thy Health CW 594

◆ ◆ ◆

I ^{1}whyles ^{2}claw the elbow o'
troublesome Thought.   sometimes scratch

◆

My mirth and guid humour are coin in my pouch.
                                    Contented wi' Little CW 532

◆ ◆ ◆

I'll act with prudence as far as I'm able.
                                    Fickle Fortune CW 56

◆ ◆ ◆

I sat me down to ponder
Upon an auld tree-root.
                                    One Night as I did Wander CW 48

◆ ◆ ◆

Is there a man, whose judgement clear
Can others teach the course to steer,
Yet runs, himself, life's mad career,
Wild as the wave?
                                    A Bard's Epitaph CW 220

◆ ◆ ◆

He'll hae misfortunes great an sma,
But ay a heart aboon them a'.   above
                                    Rantin, Rovin Robin CW 268

THE MUSE

I come to give thee such reward as we bestow.

The Scottish Muse

A wildly-witty, rustic grace
Shone full upon her.

•

I come to give thee such reward,
As we bestow!

•

I mark'd thy embryo-tuneful flame,
Thy natal hour.

•

'With future hope I oft would gaze
Fond, on thy little early ways.

•

'I saw thee seek the sounding shore,
Delighted with the dashing roar.

And joy and music pouring forth . . . .
I saw thee eye the gen'ral mirth
With boundless love.

♦

When youthful Love, warm-blushing, strong,
Keen-shivering, shot thy nerves along . . . .
I taught thee how to pour in song
To soothe thy flame.

♦

I saw thy pulse's maddening play
Wild-send thee Pleasure's devious way.

♦

Then never murmur nor repine;
Strive in thy humble sphere to shine;
And trust me.

♦

Preserve the dignity of Man,
With soul erect,
And trust the Universal Plan.

The Vision CW 116/21

♦ ♦ ♦

Though his artless strains he rudely sings . . . .
He glows with all the spirit of the bard.

The Brigs of Ayr CW 244

NATURE

The outstretched lake, imbosomed 'mong the hills.

Yet Nature's charms, the hills and woods,
The sweeping vales, and foaming floods,
Are free alike to all.

Epistle to Davie, a Brother Poet CW 87

◆ ◆ ◆

Yet, all beneath th' unrivall'd rose,
The lowly daisy sweetly blows.

The Vision CW 120

◆ ◆ ◆

Thou saw . . . . weary winter comin fast
An cozie here, beneath the blast,
Thou thought to dwell.

◆

That wee bit heap o leaves an stibble,
Has cost thee monie a weary nibble!

To a Mouse CW 132

♦ ♦ ♦

Cauld blew the bitter-biting north
Upon thy early, humble birth;
Yet cheerfully thou glinted forth
Amid the storm.

To a Mountain Daisy CW 203

♦ ♦ ♦

Ev'n winter bleak has charms to me,
When winds rave thro the naked tree.

Epistle to William Simpson CW 109

♦ ♦ ♦

The chilly frost, beneath the silver beam,
Crept, gently-crusting, o'er the glittering stream.

All-cheering Plenty, with her flowing horn,
Led yellow Autumn wreath'd with nodding corn.

The Brigs of Ayr CW 245 & 9

♦ ♦ ♦

At dawn, when every grassy blade
Droops with a diamond at his head.

Elegy on Captain Matthew Henderson CW 338

♦ ♦ ♦

As bees bizz out wi angry ¹fyke,   fuss
When plundering herds assail their ¹byke.   hive

Tam o' Shanter CW 414

◆ ◆ ◆

While Autumn, benefactor kind . . . .
. . . sees, with self-approving mind,
Each creature on his bounty fed.

Address to the Shade of Thomson CW 421

◆ ◆ ◆

Common friend to you and me,
Nature's gifts to all are free.

◆

The eagle . . . . in his breast no pity dwells,
Strong necessity compels.

On Scaring some Water-Fowl in Loch Turit CW 296

◆ ◆ ◆

Th' outstretching lake, imbosomed 'mong the hills,
The eye with wonder and amazement fills.

Verses Written with a Pencil CW 287

◆ ◆ ◆

May'st thou long, sweet crimson gem,
Richly deck thy native stem.

To Miss Cruikshank CW 368

◆ ◆ ◆

When Nature her great masterpiece design'd . . . .
She form'd of various parts the various Man.

The order'd system fair before her stood;
Nature, well pleas'd, pronounc'd it very good.

So, to heaven's gates the lark's shrill song ascends,
But grovelling on the earth the carol ends.
Epistle to Robert Graham, Esq., of Fintry CW 330/2

◆ ◆ ◆

The mavis wild wi monie a note,
Sings drowsy day to rest.
Lament of Mary Queen of Scots CW 401

◆ ◆ ◆

As blooming Spring unbends the brow
Of surly, savage Winter.
Young Peggy CW 126

◆ ◆ ◆

And gentle the fall of the soft vernal shower,
That steals on the evening each leaf to renew!
The Banks of the Devon CW 298

◆ ◆ ◆

A rose-bud, by my early walk . . . .
In a' its crimson glory spread . . . .
It scents the early morning.
A Rose-Bud, by my Early Walk CW 318

54

See yonder rosebud rich in dew . . . .
How sune it ¹tines its scent and hue,   loses
When ¹pu'd and worn.   pulled

I do Confess Thou Art Sae Fair CW 442

◆ ◆ ◆

The eagle's gaze alone surveys
The sun's meridian splendours.

Lovely Davies CW 423

◆ ◆ ◆

The happy hour may soon be near
That brings us pleasant weather.

Nithsdale's Welcome Hame CW 378

◆ ◆ ◆

And the longer it blossom'd the sweeter it grew.

Lady Mary Ann CW 460

◆ ◆ ◆

Thro gentle showers, the laughing flowers
In double pride were gay.

The Winter of Life CW 525

◆ ◆ ◆

Look abroad thro Nature's range,
Nature's mighty law is change.

Let Not Women E'er Complain CW 525

◆ ◆ ◆

At the starless, midnight hour
When Winter rules with boundless power.

On the Seas and Far Away CW 518

◆ ◆ ◆

As on the brier the budding rose
Still richer breathes and fairer blows.

Philly and Willy CW 529

◆ ◆ ◆

The primroses blow in the dews of the morning,
And wild scatter'd cowslips bedeck the green dale.

The Chevalier's Lament CW 322

◆ ◆ ◆

When day, expiring in the west,
The curtain draws o Nature's rest.

Dainty Davie CW 499

PATRIOTISM

*Old poets have sung and
old chronicles tell.*

*Yet let my country need me . . . .
I'd clatter on my stumps at the sound of the drum.*
                                        The Jolly Beggars CW 183

◆ ◆ ◆

*A well-known land . . .
Here, rivers in the sea were lost;
There, mountains to the skies were toss't.*

◆

*I mark'd a martial race, pourtray'd
In colours strong.*

                                        The Vision CW 116/7

◆ ◆ ◆

From scenes like these, old Scotia's grandeur springs,
That makes her lov'd at home, rever'd abroad.

The Cotter's Saturday Night CW 150

◆ ◆ ◆

But mark the Rustic, haggis-fed,
The trembling earth resounds his tread.

Address to a Haggis CW 265

◆ ◆ ◆

Whose ancestors, in days of yore,
Thro hostile ranks and ruin'd gaps
Old Scotia's bloody lion bore.

Address to Edinburgh CW 263

◆ ◆ ◆

And the foe you cannot brave,
Scorn at least to be his slave.

On Scaring Some Water-Fowl In Loch Turit CW 297

◆ ◆ ◆

Lang may she stand to prop the land,   Caledonia
The flow'r of ancient nations.

Nature's Law CW 254

◆ ◆ ◆

The rough burr-thistle spreading wide . . . .
I turn'd the weeder-clips aside,
An' spar'd the symbol dear.

To the Guidwife of Wauchope House CW 271

But here an ancient nation, fam'd afar
For genius, learning high, as great in war.
Hail, Caledonia! name forever dear!

•

Where every science, every nobler art,
That can inform the mind or mend the heart,
Is known.

•

Here History paints with elegance and force
The tide of Empire's fluctuating course.

Prologue Spoken by Mr Woods CW 275

◆ ◆ ◆

No song nor dance I bring from yon great city . . . .
Good sense and taste are natives here at home.

Prologue Spoken at the Theatre of Dumfries CW 376

◆ ◆ ◆

Lead on the unmuzzled hounds of Hell,
Till all the frightened echoes tell
The blood-notes of the chase!

Birthday Ode for 31st December, 1787 CW 304

◆ ◆ ◆

Thee, Caledonia . . . .
To thee I turn with swimming eyes!
Where is that soul of Freedom fled?

Ode for General Washington's Birthday CW 516

◆ ◆ ◆

And for my dear-lov'd Land o Cakes,
I pray with holy fire.

Election Ballad CW 406

◆ ◆ ◆

Revers'd that spear redoubtable in war,
Reclined that banner, ¹erst in fields unfurl'd. formerly

Elegy on the Death of Sir James Hunter Blair CW 282

◆ ◆ ◆

In Heaven itself I'll ask no more
Than just a Highland welcome.

A Highland Welcome CW 292

◆ ◆ ◆

The Stewarts all were brave . . . . but fools,
Not one of them a knave.

Epigrams against the Earl of Galloway CW 494

◆ ◆ ◆

Old poets have sung, and old chronicles tell,
What champions ventur'd, what champions fell.

◆

And, knee-deep in claret, he'd die ere he'd yield.

The Whistle CW 368/9

◆ ◆ ◆

Untie these bands from off my hands,
And bring to me my sword.

◆

May coward shame distain his name,
The wretch that dare not die!

Macpherson's Farewell CW 308

♦ ♦ ♦

Honour's war we strongly waged,
But the heavens deny'd success.

Strathallan's Lament CW 287

♦ ♦ ♦

Come weal, come woe, we'll gather and go,
And live or die wi Charlie!

♦

If I had twenty thousand lives,
I'd die as aft for Charlie!

O'er the Water to Charlie CW 316

♦ ♦ ♦

Go, teach them to tremble, fell tyrant, but know,
No terrors hast thou to the brave.

The Song of Death CW 420

♦ ♦ ♦

The wretch that would a tyrant own . . . .
May they be damn'd together!

Does Haughty Gaul Invasion Threat? CW 538

♦ ♦ ♦

When wild War's deadly blast was blawn,
And gentle Peace returning.

The Soldier's Return CW 487

See approach proud Edward's power -
Chains and slaverie!

Wha sae base as be a slave?
Let him turn and flee!

We will drain our dearest veins,
But they shall be free!

Scots, Wha hae CW 500

Far dearer to me yon lone glen o green breckan,
Wi' the burn stealing under the lang, yellow broom.

Their Groves o' Sweet Myrtle CW 550

A lambkin in peace but a lion in war. Caledonia

Caledonia CW 349

FEAR

In Hell they'll roast thee like a herrin'.

But och! I backward cast my e'e
On prospects drear,
An forward, tho I canna see,
I guess an fear.

To a Mouse CW 132

♦♦♦

The fear o Hell's a hangman's whip.

Epistle to a Young Friend CW 222

♦♦♦

I tremble to approach an angry God.

Stanzas on the Same Occasion CW 54

♦♦♦

Deil tak the hindmost, on they drive.

Address to a Haggis CW 264

♦♦♦

That night, a child might understand,
The Deil had business on his hand.

In hell they'll roast thee like a herrin!

Tam o' Shanter CW 411 & 414

♦ ♦ ♦

To think how we stood sweatin, shakin,
An pish'd wi dread.

Holly Willie's Prayer CW 95

♦ ♦ ♦

Satan, I fear thy sooty claws,
I hate thy brunstane stink.

To William Stewart CW 351

GRIEF

An' down the briny pearls rowe.

(A Bard) In loud lament bewail'd his lord,
Whom Death had all untimely ta'en.

•

But ¹nocht in all revolving time   nothing
Can gladness bring again to me.

•

I am a bending aged tree,
That long has stood the wind and rain.

•

For silent, low, on beds of dust,
Lie a' that would my sorrows share.

Lament for James, Earl of Glencairn CW 423/4

• • •

An down the briny pearls rowe
For Mailie dead.

Poor Mailie's Elegy CW 65

❖ ❖ ❖

But some day ye may gnaw your nails,
An curse your folly sairly.

A Dream CW 235

❖ ❖ ❖

In durance vile here must I wake and weep.

From Esopus to Maria CW 540

❖ ❖ ❖

Low lies the hand that oft was stretch'd to save,
Low lies the heart that swell'd with honor's pride.

Elegy on the Death of Sir James Hunter Blair CW 282

❖ ❖ ❖

How slow ye move, ye heavy hours!
The joyless day how dreary!

How Lang and Dreary is the Night CW 524

❖ ❖ ❖

Gentle night, do thou befriend me!
Downy sleep, the curtain draw!

Musing on the Roaring Ocean CW 315

❖ ❖ ❖

When remembrance wracks the mind,
Pleasures but unveil despair.

Frae the Friends and Land I Love CW 437

Time cannot aid me, my griefs are immortal,
Not Hope dare a comfort bestow.

Where are the Joys CW 505

♦ ♦ ♦

Ye tempests, rage! ye turbid torrents, roll!
Ye suit the joyless tenor of my soul.

On the Death of Lord President Dundas CW 301

♦ ♦ ♦

Ye rugged cliffs o'erhanging dreary glens,
To you I fly: ye with my soul accord.

Elegy on the late Miss Burnet of Monboddo CW 416

SUPPLICATION

O Lord yestreen, thou kens, wi' Meg.

O wad some Power the giftie gie us
To see oursels as ithers see us!

To a Louse CW 182

• • •

But yet, O Lord! confess I must,
At times I'm ¹*fash'd wi fleshly lust.*   troubled

•

O Lord! yestreen, Thou kens, wi Meg -
Thy pardon I sincerely beg . . . .
An I'll ne'er lift a lawless leg
Again upon her.

•

Lord, hear my earnest cry and pray'r.

•

But, Lord, remember me and mine
Wi' mercies temporal and divine.

Holy Willie's Prayer CW 93/5

♦ ♦ ♦

Through and through th' inspir'd leaves,
Ye maggots, make your windings;
But O, respect his lordship's taste,
And spare the golden bindings!

The Bookworms CW 608

♦ ♦ ♦

May never worse be sent;
But, whether granted or denied,
Lord, bless us with content.

A Grace Before Dinner CW 363

♦ ♦ ♦

Peace, thy olive wand extend
And bid wild War his ravage end.

On the Seas and Far Away CW 518

♦ ♦ ♦

Then let us pray that come it may . . . .
That man to man the world, o'er
Shall brithers be for a' that.

A Man's a Man for A' That CW 536

POLITICS & SOCIETY

Highlandmen hate tolls an'taxes

Princes and lords are but the breath of kings,
'An honest man's the noblest work of God.

◆

Then however crowns and coronets be rent,
A virtuous populace may rise the while.

The Cotter's Saturday Night CW 150/1

◆ ◆ ◆

Courts for cowards were erected,
Churches built to please the priest!

The Jolly Beggars CW 191

◆ ◆ ◆

An buirdly ¹chiels, an clever ²hizzies, stalwart men, women
Are bred in ¹sic a way as this is. such

◆

The dearest comfort o their lives,
Their ¹grushie ²weans an faithfu wives. robust (or sturdy) children

◆

An ay the less they hae to ¹sturt them, fret
In like proportion, less will hurt them.

The Twa Dogs CW 142/5

◆ ◆ ◆

The thresher's weary flingin-tree, flail
The lee-lang day had tired me.

The Vision CW 115

◆ ◆ ◆

I'm truly sorry man's dominion
Has broken Nature's social union.

To a Mouse CW 131

◆ ◆ ◆

It's hardly in a body's pow'r,
To keep, at times, frae being sour,
To see how things are shar'd.

Epistle to Davie, a Brother Poet CW 86

◆ ◆ ◆

'A few seem favourites of Fate,
In pleasure's lap carest.

•

Man's·inhumanity to man
Makes countless thousands mourn!

Man was Made to Mourn CW 124

♦ ♦ ♦

Were this the charter of our state,
'On pain o hell be rich an great,'
Damnation then would be our fate,
Beyond remead.

Second Epistle to J Lapraik CW 106

♦ ♦ ♦

. . . Highlandmen hate tolls an taxes.

Epistle to William Simpson CW 109

♦ ♦ ♦

What warm, poetic heart but inly bleeds,
And execrates man's savage, ruthless deeds!

The Brigs of Ayr CW 245

♦ ♦ ♦

'O ye! who, sunk in beds of down,
Feel not a want but what yourselves create.

A Winter Night CW 260

♦ ♦ ♦

Foxes and statesmen subtile wiles ensure;
The cit and polecat stink, and are secure.

To Robert Graham, Esq., of Fintry CW 431

◆ ◆ ◆

O, why has Worth so short a date,
While villains ripen grey with time!

Lament for James, Earl of Glencairn CW 425

◆ ◆ ◆

Of what enjoyments thou hast ¹reft us!   taken from
In what a pickle thou hast left us!

Elegy on the Year 1788 CW 347

◆ ◆ ◆

The doctrine to-day, that is loyalty sound,
To-morrow may bring us a halter!

Address to Wm. Tytler, Esq., of Woodhouselee CW 276

◆ ◆ ◆

Doom'd to that sorest task of man alive -
To make three guineas do the work of five.

Address Spoken by Miss Fontenelle CW 509

◆ ◆ ◆

No Babel-structure would I build . . . .
While all would rule and none obey.

Ode on the Departed Regency Bill CW 353

◆ ◆ ◆

Mark ruffian Violence, distained with crimes,
Rousing elate in these degenerate times!

◆

. . . Litigation's pliant tongue
The life-blood equal sucks of Right and Wrong!

On the Death of Lord President Dundas CW 301

◆ ◆ ◆

And with sincere, tho unavailing, sighs
I view the helpless children of distress.

Tragic Fragment CW 46

◆ ◆ ◆

Ye hypocrites! . . . .
To murder men, and give God thanks?
Desist for shame!

Thanksgiving for a National Victory CW 485

◆ ◆ ◆

What force or guile could not subdue . . . .
Is wrought now by a coward few.

Such a Parcel of Rogues in a Nation CW 461

◆ ◆ ◆

For never but by British hands
¹Maun British wrangs be righted!   Must

Does Haughty Gaul Invasion Threat CW 537

◆ ◆ ◆

For gold the merchant ploughs the main,
The farmer ploughs the manor.

The Soldier's Return CW 488

◆ ◆ ◆

O, wae be to you, Men o State,
That brethren rouse in deadly hate!

Logan Braes CW 491

◆ ◆ ◆

The rank is but the guinea's stamp,
The man's the ¹gowd for a' that.   gold

◆

A prince can mak a belted knight . . . .
But an honest man's ¹aboon his might-   above

A Man's a Man for A' That CW 535/6

◆ ◆ ◆

The Kirk an State may gae to Hell,
And I'll gae to my Anna.

Yestreen I had a Pint o' Wine CW 408

MORALITY

*O ye wha are sae
guid yersel.*

But, och! mankind are ¹*unco weak,*   very
An little to be trusted.

Epistle to a Young Friend CW 221

◆ ◆ ◆

Some books are lies frae end to end,
And some great lies were never penn'd.

Death and Doctor Hornbook CW 96

◆ ◆ ◆

O ye, wha are sae guid yoursel,
Sae pious and sae holy.

◆

Then gently scan your brother man,
Still gentler sister woman;
Tho they may gang a kennin wrang,
To step aside is human.

•

What's done we partly may compute,
But know not what's resisted.

Address to the Unco Guid CW 74 & 76

• • •

Say, to be just, and kind, and wise -
There solid self-enjoyment lies.

•

That foolish, selfish, faithless ways
Lead to be wretched, vile, and base.

Written in Friars Carse Hermitage CW 326

• • •

With passions so potent, and fancies so bright,
No man with the half of 'em e'er could go right.

•

No two virtues, whatever relation they claim . . . .
Possessing the one shall imply you've the other.

Inscribed to the Right Hon C.J. Fox CW 357

FAITH

*Thou giv'st the ass his hide,
the snail his shell.*

*They never sought in vain that sought
the Lord aright.*

The Cotter's Saturday Night CW 148

◆ ◆ ◆

*But, Thou art good; and Goodness still
Delighteth to forgive.*

A Prayer in the Prospect of Death CW 54

◆ ◆ ◆

*A correspondence fix'd wi' Heav'n
Is sure a noble anchor!*

Epistle to a Young Friend CW 222

◆ ◆ ◆

Who made the heart, 'tis He alone
Decidedly can try us.

Address to the Unco Guid CW 76

◆ ◆ ◆

The heart benevolent and kind
The most resembles God.

A Winter Night CW 260

◆ ◆ ◆

Thy nod can make the tempest cease to blow,
Or still the tumult of the raging sea.

Stanzas, On the Same Occasion CW 55

◆ ◆ ◆

But hath decreed that wicked men
Shall ne'er be truly blest.

Paraphrase of the First Psalm CW 57

◆ ◆ ◆

O Thou Great Being! what Thou art
Surpasses me to know.

Prayer under the Pressure of Violent Anguish CW 55

◆ ◆ ◆

The cave-lodged beggar, with a conscience clear,
Expires in rags, unknown, and goes to Heaven.

Ode, Sacred to the Memory of Mrs Oswald of Auchencruive CW 343

◆ ◆ ◆

Thou giv'st the ass his hide, the snail his shell.
To Robert Graham, Esq., of Fintry CW 431

◆ ◆ ◆

O Thou that in the Heavens does dwell . . . .
Sends ane to Heaven, an ten to Hell.
Holy Willie's Prayer CW 93

◆ ◆ ◆

Reverence with lowly heart
Him, whose wondrous work thou art.
Verses in Friars' Carse Hermitage CW 324

◆ ◆ ◆

Th' ungodly o'er the just prevail'd . . . .
That Thou might'st greater glory give
Unto thine own anointed!
A New Psalm for the Chapel of Kilmarnock CW 355

◆ ◆ ◆

A heretic blast has been blawn i' the Wast,
That what is not sense must be nonsense.
The Kirk's Alarm CW 359

◆ ◆ ◆

My helpless lambs, I trust them wi him. pet ewe speaks
The Death and Dying Words of Poor Mailie CW 63

◆ ◆ ◆

Which shows that Heaven can boil the pot,
Tho the Deil piss in the fire.
The Dean of the Faculty CW 562